CPSIA information can be obtained
at www.ICGtesting.com
Printed in the USA
LVHW101140170423
744536LV00004B/206

9 781669 520474